AF572038

HASIDIM

The Trees Still Bloom

ISBN – D-915361-88-4
Printed in Israel

Design – Yoav Graphica. Typesetting – EL-OT Ltd. Printing – Tal Press

JOEL KANTOR / YOEL RAPPEL
Photographs / Text

ADAMA BOOKS

Waiting for the Messiah

In the earliest days of the Hasidic movement (which was founded in the mid-18th century) – before it became a mass movement – its ties to *Eretz Israel* were established. One can find expression of this in the remarkable stories of the voyage of the founder of the movement, Rabbi Israel Baal Shem Tov, to the Promised Land; a trip which was never completed due to various obstructions along the way. From that time until today, the love of the land of Israel and the duty to immigrate to it have been cardinal principles of the Hasidism.

It was to the credit of the Hasidic movement that it always stressed the commandment to live in *Eretz Israel,* a commandment that had been neglected for many generations. The *aliyah* – immigration – of the first Hasidim, who came with their illustrious leaders to *Eretz Israel,* drew from two main sources: on the one hand, the movement was influenced by kabbalistic sources, primarily that of the *Ari,* which were strongly tied to *Eretz Israel* and which resulted in Hasidic striving to draw the redemption closer by "practical" means. On the other hand, the Hasidim wanted to establish a new center for their movement in *Eretz Israel,* a center which would be sanctified by the holiness of the land and would in turn radiate its influence outward. This was to a large extent a reaction to the sharp opposition in the diaspora against Hasidism.

In addition, Hasidism was vitally concerned with hastening the coming of the Messiah, not only by repentance and prayer, but also by developing a large Jewish presence in the Holy Land. This was expressed by the foremost Hasidic scholars and kabbalists who came to the country, and who regarded their immigration to the land as part of their Messianic belief. Beyond that, the very act of coming to the land was seen as a way of perfecting one's Judaism. There is no doubt that the sanctity of the land and the ability to observe all the commandments in it (something impossible outside it) was the main motivation of these Hasidim.

The spiritual centrality of *Eretz Israel* in the philosphy of Hasidism was expressed in Hasidic stories and parables. The Maggid of Mezrich said: *"Zion is the main focus of the world, and it is it that keeps the world alive."* Rabbi Israel of Polotsk wrote from *Eretz Israel: "Our precious land, precious to our hearts, the joy of our thoughts, the most sanctified of all sanctities."* And Rabbi Mordechai of Lachowicze put it this way: *"Whoever lives in Eretz Israel is considered to be righteous."*

Given these statements, it was natural that the Hasidic leaders went to the greatest of lengths to move to the land and settle in it, or at least to visit it and to imbibe of its sanctity.

The impetus to move began at the time of the Baal Shem Tov, the founder of Hasidism. The first Hasid to immigrate was Rabbi Gershon of Kosov, who arrived in *Eretz Israel* in 1746. Two of the Baal Shem Tov's close disciples, Rabbi

Menahem Mendl of Premyshlan and Rabbi Nahman of Horodenka, led a group of thirty people, who arrived in the country in 1764. A major turning point in the Hasidic immigration to the Holy Land occurred in 1777, when a few hundred Hasidim, led by Rabbi Menahem Mendl of Vitebsk, Rabbi Abraham Hakohen of Kalisz, and Rabbi Israel of Polotsk, arrived. From that year on, there was a constant Hasidic influx to the Holy Land, sometimes by complete groups, other times by individuals who made their way across the ocean, seeing in their move an opportunity to settle the land and thereby to help preserve the Jewish people.

By the very act of immigration to *Eretz Israel,* the Hasidim opened a new page in the history of the Jews of Eastern Europe – then the largest Jewish concentration in the world – and it was they who renewed the Ashkenazic community in the country. And Hasidism, as any national religious group, soon developed an ideology and rationale for the course that it expected each individual to follow, which should ultimately bring him to settle in the Holy Land.

But not every person is suitable for or able to settle in *Eretz Israel.* The difficult conditions which greeted the new immigrants, and the duty to make a public declaration of faith, which is required by anyone living in the Lord's own land, dissuaded many Hasidim from making the trip.

It is told: *"When Rabbi Menahem Mendl of Kotsk's disciples came to him to request permission to move to Eretz Israel, he told them, 'I never realized how much you care for your own selves.'"* In general, Rabbi Menahem Mendl did not advise his disciples to move to the Holy Land, telling them *"Haven't you sinned enough in your own homes that you wish to sin in the palace of the King? In your youth, when you would have been able to be involved in the rebuilding and settling of the land, you did not make the move. Now that you are old and weak, you wish to go to Eretz Israel. The Torah has already informed us that 'your carcasses will die in this desert.' If you really wish to fulfill a commandment, send your children to Eretz Israel."*

Those who visited *Eretz Israel* and those who settled there saw themselves as representing their communities. Thus, when returning from such a visit, or when they happened to meet other Hasidim, they felt themselves duty-bound to tell only the good of the country, so as to encourage others to follow their lead.

The move to *Eretz Israel* and the building of the Jewish settlement there were both due to the fact that *Eretz Israel* was the Holy Land. Rabbi Nahman of Bratslav arrived in *Eretz Israel* in 1799, the year that Napoleon was conducting his campaign to conquer Palestine. Of that time, Rabbi Nahman wrote, *"When I was in Eretz Israel, I heard from prominent people that before they had come to Eretz Israel they*

couldn't imagine that it belongs to our world. Based on what they had read in the holy books about its sanctity, they were convinced that it was entirely on a different plane. However, after they came to Eretz Israel they found that it is indeed in this world. Its earth is just like the earth of all countries from which they came. Its outward appearance is no different than that of other countries – and yet, it is the most holy of all countries. This is similar to the truly righteous person, the tzaddik, *who appears outwardly to be the same as everyone else. The* tzaddik *is nevertheless different, but only those who believe in him can sense his holiness. In the same way, only those who believe in the sanctity of Eretz Israel can feel its holiness and can realize that its skies are different."*

To the Hasidim, *Eretz Israel* is the epitome of perfection, lacking nothing, and it is to it that all must strive to come, so as to await the Messiah and the ultimate redemption. It is told that the Rabbi of Stretin, who all his life longed for the ultimate redemption and to settle in *Eretz Israel,* died not because of illness, but because he pined away for the Messiah, so that his soul simply was unable to survive.

Eretz Israel was at the center of Rabbi Nahman of Bratslav's Torah teachings: *"My place is only in Eretz Israel."* The young leader, who was but 26 years old, and was a great-grandson of the Baal Shem Tov, wanted to absorb the holiness of *Eretz Israel,* so as to be able to impart that spirit to others. As he put it, *"The source of wisdom is in Eretz Israel."* His trip there was the dominant event of his life. It is only thus that we can understand his stubbornness when he was destitute, sick, and coughing up blood, to abandon his family and to set off on his journey to *Eretz Israel.*

Rabbi Nahman of Bratslav's journey, as described by his disciple, Rabbi Nathan, has been reprinted scores of times in various Hasidic works, and made a deep impact on the movement and its longing for *Eretz Israel.* Many of the Hasidim became very attached to the land, for Rabbi Nahman had said: *"Whoever wishes to be a true Jew, whether old or young, must gird himself and come to Eretz Israel, for the sanctity of Eretz Israel is enough for all of us. That is our home. That is our country. That is our soil. That is our fate. And outside Eretz Israel we are like visitors who are resting for a while."*

Rabbi Nahman of Bratslav did not remain in *Eretz Israel.* His return to the diaspora did not signify a failure to "make it." The *tzaddik,* who longed for his disciples who had remained in the Ukraine, worked hard at implanting a love of the country and at raising funds for those living in it. His disciples followed in his footsteps to the extent that after his death they refused to look for another leader to replace him. After all, Rabbi Nahman had stated, *"My light will not be extinguished until the Redeemer arrives."*

***

During the 19th century, there was a constant influx of Hasidim into *Eretz Israel*. The new immigrants included great Torah scholars and community leaders who brought their communities with them. It is worth mentioning Rabbi Issachar Ber of Zalozhtsy and Rabbi David Solomon Eibenschutz (author of *Levushei Serad*), who immigrated from Jassy to Safed in 1809. Four years later, in 1813, Rabbi Solomon of Tchernowitz, known for his *Be'er Mayim Ha'im* commentary, also arrived in the country. During this period, a whole group of Karlin Hasidim came, led by Rabbi Jacob Karlin, and they were joined by Hasidim of Slonim. A great scholar was Rabbi Abraham Dov of Ovruch, who became known as the leader of the Hasidim in Safed. It was he who revived the spirit of the community in that city. Rabbi Abraham Dov of Ovruch became known for his great deeds following the earthquake in Safed in 1837. The earthquake, and the riots by the Druze in the following year, brought about the collapse of that community, which suffered hundreds of dead and wounded. There is no doubt that Rabbi Abraham Dov's leadership was the one factor which kept it from total chaos.

But even Rabbi Abraham Dov's powers were limited; when the most famous Hasid in Safed, Rabbi Nissan Bek, the renowned printer, decided to move to Jerusalem, that was the beginning of a decline of which historians tell us: *"Jerusalem was built on the ruins of Safed."* And indeed, the blows that hit Safed between 1834 and 1839 brought about the foundation of the Hasidic center in Jerusalem.

It was because of this transfusion of scholars that from 1845 on the Jerusalem Hasidic *kolel* – the institute for higher Jewish learning – became an independent entity.

***

The constant inflow of Hasidim into *Eretz Israel* served to enrich the spiritual life of the community, but had very little influence on the development of the country as such. The dependence of most Jews on the *halukah*, the charitable disbursement of funds raised abroad, and the lack of any trades which might support a family, affected the Hasidic centers in the four main cities: Safed, Tiberias, Jerusalem, and Hebron. There is no doubt that the deep longing for *Eretz Israel* and the strong spiritual ties to its sanctity shown by the Hasidim were responsible for the phenomenal ability of the Hasidim to deal with all the difficulties that they faced.

Things changed completely with the beginning of the Zionist movement. During the first, second and third *aliyah* periods (1882-1924), the Hasidim who came to the country did so with the goal of setting up new settlements and of participating in the rebirth of the national home in *Eretz Israel*.

In 1922 a group of Hasidim, led by Rabbi Isaac Gershtenkorn, immigrated from Poland and laid the foundations for what in those days was the Bnei Brak moshav settlement. This later became a vibrant city, with a population of tens of thousands. Among those early settlers, who had to undergo all types of trials and tribulations, were many Hasidim of the Gur Hasidic court; and their leader, Rabbi Abraham Mordechai Alter, not only preached on the importance of moving to *Eretz Israel* but served as a personal example by doing so himself. He himself travelled back and forth between Poland and *Eretz Israel* six times, until he finally settled in Bnei Brak in 1939.

At the initiative of Rabbi Israel Hopstein and Rabbi Ezekiel Taub, a group was organized in Poland of Hasidim who had suffered terribly in the economic depression and the prevalent climate of anti-Semitism in that country. These Hasidim decided to liquidate all their assets in Poland and organized to set up a new settlement in *Eretz Israel,* where they would earn their living as farmers. In the years 1925 and 1926, 110 Hasidic families immigrated to *Eretz Israel* and settled in Emek Zevulun, where they established Kfar Hasidim – another attempt of the Hasidic world, following the establishment of Bnei Brak, to open an agricultural settlement. This agricultural experiment succeeded even though the settlers did not receive the financial support of the Jewish *Yishuv* – the organized Jewish community in *Eretz Israel* at the time. Their enthusiasm, their faith, and their spiritual attachment to the soil obscured any feeling of deprivation that they might have suffered.

Twenty-five years later, in 1949, a group of Hasidim who were refugees from Russia organized and established, at the direction of the Lubavicher Rebbe, Rabbi Joseph Isaac Schneerson, a settlement which they named Kfar Habad. Their remarkable faith in the Jewish heritage and traditions had enabled them to survive the persecution in Russia and gave them the strength of character to set up a thriving community.

After the establishment of the State of Israel, a number of Hasidic rabbis organized to set up communities for their own followers. The first of these was Rabbi Haim Meir Hager of Vizhnitz, who set up a beautiful neighborhood in Bnei Brak. Afterwards, in 1956, the Sanz-Klausenberg district was established in Netanyah, in what is known today as Kiryat Sanz. The district, which contains hundreds of families, was built when the Klausenberger rabbi declared: *"Every Jew outside Eretz Israel who observes the commandments is duty-bound to observe the verse, 'the sons shall return to their borders.'"* The district contains magnificent Torah institutions, a hospital, a hotel, an old-age home, and other such facilities.

The district of Netanyah has served as a model for similar districts. From the time that the Hasidim became citizens of the State of Israel, they spread into various towns, and in each case maintained the unique framework which has enabled them to hold on to their personal ways, while at the same time being part and parcel of the larger city. The Gur Hasidim have set up districts in Hazor, Arad, Ashdod, and Tel Aviv. At the initiative of Rabbi Solomon Halberstam, the Bobover Hasidim established their district in Bat Yam. The Krechnev Hasidim built a district in Rehovot, while Karlin turned to the new city of Emmanuel. The Sasov Hasidim constructed Kiryat Yismah Moshe in Kiron, while those of Bratslav returned to the town of Safed, building up their center in the old part of the town. But it is Jerusalem that remains the Torah center.

This book, *Hasidim, The Trees Still Bloom,* documents a world that once existed and still exists. The book began with a trip through Galilee, and a car drive on the Acre-Safed road. Along the way, Joel Kantor saw a group of Hasidim gathering near a tree, and he photographed the group. He was also curious to find out what the meeting was all about. The answer was simple but full of faith. One of the Hasidim said to him: "This tree has Divine properties, and each person is taking a leaf or small branch in the hope that his income will be adequate as a result." Over the course of time, the tree has gradually broken down, and it will eventually disappear. This event at the tomb of Rabbi Judah Bar Ila'i aroused his curiosity.

During 1980 and 1981, Joel Kantor was in Jerusalem studying photography. He would spend his free time walking through the ultra-Orthodox neighborhoods of Jerusalem. He always walked alone and carried a camera. He became part of the local scene, without intruding in the daily events. And thus, without their realizing it and without drawing attention to himself, he devoted his time to documenting the lives of the Hasidim. Before his eyes stood the book, *A Vanished World,* whose images documented the extinct communities of Eastern Europe, and now he had discovered that the same world still existed, at least in Jerusalem.

The photographs in this book reflect the life in the Hasidic courts in Jerusalem and Safed. These are the courts of communities that established their homes in the Holy Land and which became an integral part of its human landscape. The lives of the Hasidim are part and parcel of the life of the State of Israel. There are among them some who are extremists and some who are more moderate, but all together have a certain spark and a love of the Land of Israel.

The stories that were gathered together here and interwoven with the pictures were derived from various sources, some from primary sources and others from collections of Hasidic stories. All of them have of course been edited by the compiler. All of the stories are meant to express the spirit of Hasidism and to enhance the story told by each photograph.

Yoel Rappel

צדקה

A certain Hasid came to Rabbi Abraham of Stretin and asked him for a formula to become God-fearing. "A formula to become God-fearing?" said the rabbi, "I don't have one. But I do have a formula to achieve love of heaven."

"That's even better," responded the Hasid in great joy, "because our Sages tell us that love of heaven is even greater than fear of heaven."

"If so," said the rabbi, "Go and teach yourself to love your fellow Jews, for there is no better formula than that to achieve love of heaven."

בצלצלי שמע
וכנור

The Maggid said to his student, Rabbi Zusya: "I will not teach you the ten major principles of how to serve God, but you may learn them all from an infant and from a thief. Three things can be learned from an infant:

- He does not need any motivation to act;
- He does not stay idle for even an instant;
- Whatever he is lacking, he knows to ask for forcibly.

And seven things from a thief:

- He works at night;
- If he does not accomplish what he wished one night, he will try again the next one;
- He and his friends love one another;
- Whatever he stole is worth nothing to him, and he sells it for pennies;
- He is beaten and made to suffer, yet doesn't say a word;
- He is willing to endanger his life for that which appears trivial to others;
- He loves his beliefs, and will not exchange them for any other."

Rabbi Solomon of Karlin told:
"Why did the evil Haman wish to destroy, kill and liquidate all the Jews on one day? Wouldn't it be better to take a few days, so that each day would bring a new decree? The reason for his edict was his intense hatred for the Jews. He said to himself: 'If what I am planning for the Jews falls through and they make this a holiday for future generations, I want them to celebrate only a single day.'"

Rabbi Simha Bunim of Pshischa would tell his students: "On *Purim* the Jews get dressed up as gentiles – they drink and get drunk. On *Yom Kippur*, the 'gentiles' act as Jews. Even those who do not act as Jews the whole year fast on that day, covering themselves with a *tallit* – prayer shawl – and standing in prayer.

"But *Purim* is a greater day than *Yom Kippur*, because on *Yom Kippur* we must only afflict our bodies, whereas on *Purim* our Sages tell us that we must get totally drunk, so that we don't know the difference between praising Mordechai and cursing Haman. Is there any greater affliction than that of afflicting one's mind?"

Once on *Simhat Torah*, when Jews rejoice at the completion of the Torah reading cycle, Rabbi Naftali Zvi of Roptchitz came to the study hall. He came with some Hasidim and found other Hasidim already there whose singing could be heard from afar. The Hasidim already present greeted him with song and with a bottle of liquor. They said, "In the future, too, we will go to greet the Messiah with a bottle of liquor in our hands, to show him how we survived the bitter exile." Rabbi Naftali Zvi told them: "We will not go to greet the Messiah with a bottle of liquor, but with the Torah we have studied, and we will show him how this sweetened our bitter exile. A drop of drink is nevertheless a good thing, because it revives the soul."

One cannot be a man of truth unless one isolates oneself from others.

Rabbi Phinchas of Koretz said: "When a person sings and cannot raise his voice, and then along comes another to sing with him and raises his voice, then the first, too, can raise his voice. This is the secret of one soul clinging to another."

Once the Seer of Lublin went past a study hall and saw a great light emanating from it. He thought this must be because there were Jews inside devoutly studying Torah texts. When he went inside, he found there were two Jews inside telling one another stories of the great Hasidic rabbis.

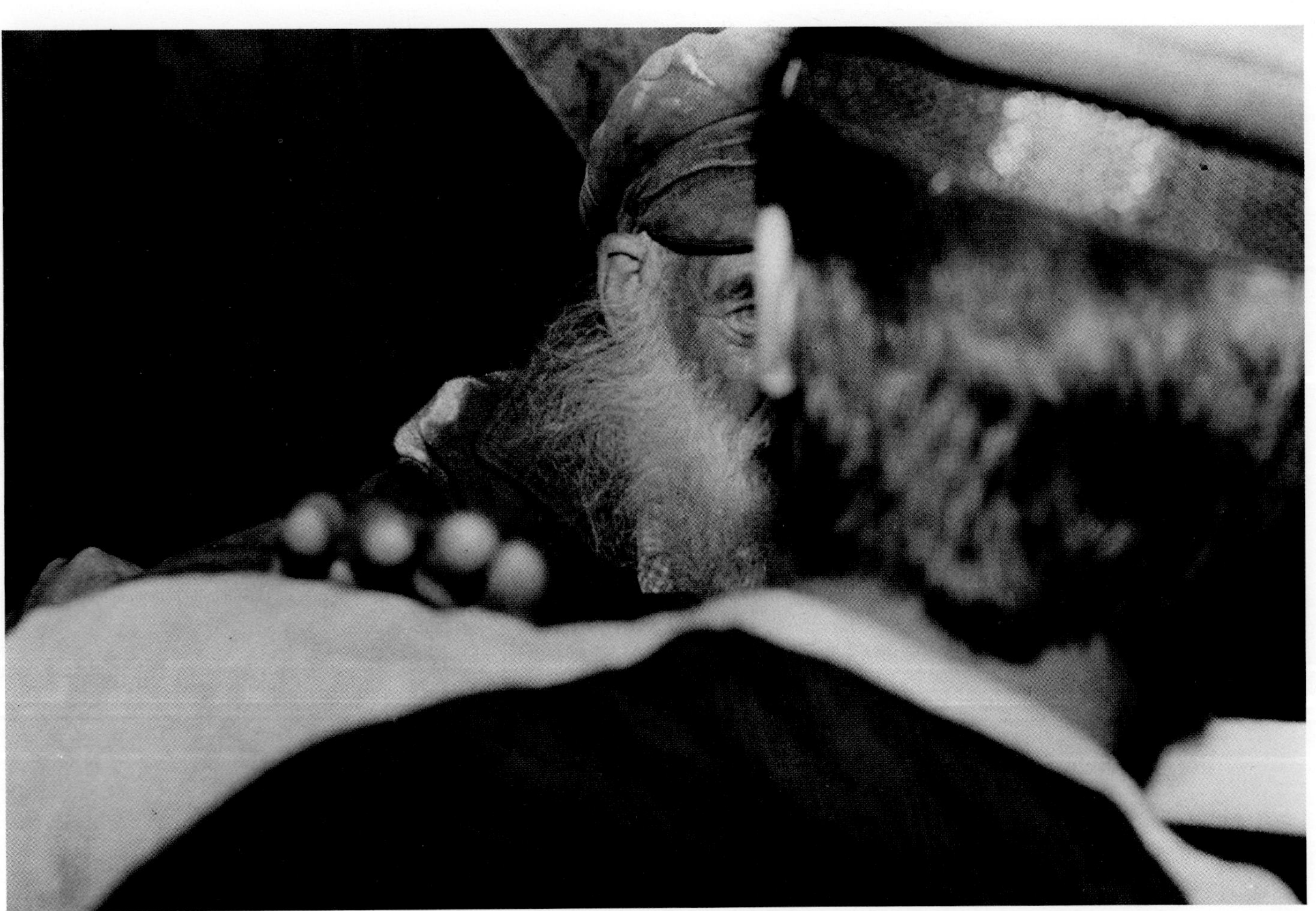

The grandson of Rabbi Baruch of Mezrich was playing hide-and-seek with his friend. He hid himself well and expected his friend to look for him. After waiting for a long time in his hiding place, he left it but found that his friend had run away without even trying to find him. The child began crying bitterly and ran to his grandfather to complain about how bad his friend was. Rabbi Baruch too began weeping and said: "That is exactly what God says. 'I hide Myself, but no one wants to look for Me.'"

While she kneaded the dough and baked, Perl, the wife of Rabbi Levi Isaac of Berdichev, would intone the following prayer: "Lord of the Universe! I beg of you – please help me so that when my Levi Isaac recites the blessing on these *hallot* that I am now baking, he should have the same lofty thoughts that I have while baking them."

When Rabbi Velvele of Zbaraz moved to the Land of Israel, his wife preferred to become a washerwoman in order to support the family, rather than to live off charity. Once Rabbi Jacob Samson of Sheptivka came for a visit. As he approached their home, he saw Rabbi Velvele's wife scrubbing the wash outside. Feeling how humiliating it must be for the wife of a prominent rabbi to have to do her wash in public, Rabbi Jacob Samson decided to leave so that he would not cause the couple humiliation.

At that moment, Rabbi Velvele's wife spotted him; she immediately felt his discomfort. "Do not be concerned, Rabbi," she told him. "This is not my personal wash, but rather work that I undertake, and which ensures our livelihood. Thank God that we are able to live in *Eretz Israel* and live off our manual labor."

Rabbi Jacob Samson entered their home and greeted Rabbi Velvele with great joy.

At a time when the Jews were in great distress, the Rabbi of Apta, who was then the elder rabbi of the generation, ordered that everyone should fast so as to arouse God's mercy. Rabbi Israel, though, called upon his musicians, whom he had assembled with great diligence, and ordered them to play on his balcony their choicest tunes each night. Whenever the beautiful music of the pipes and cymbals was heard, the Hasidim would gather together and the melody would soon dispel their sadness. Soon all would be dancing and clapping hands.
Others saw what was happening and were furious. They came to the Rabbi of Apta and told him how the fast that he had decreed had been converted into a mass celebration. The rabbi answered them: "I will not argue with the man who remembered the commandment of the Torah: 'When you must wage war in your land when an enemy besieges you, you shall blow the pipes and be remembered before the Lord your God'" (Numbers 10:9).

Joy without thinking is just revelry.

Rabbi Yehiel of Zalozhtsy once visited a certain town where he had never been before. The dignitaries of the town came to greet him. The *tzaddik* – Hasidic leader – looked at each man's forehead and told him what his spiritual faults were, and how to cure them. Within a short time the rumor went about the entire town that the *tzaddik* was able to read people's faces and to tell from them everyone's character. People then began having second thoughts about meeting him. Those who did come, pushed their caps over their heads so as to cover their entire forehead to their nose. "You are mistaken," Rabbi Yehiel told them. "An eye that can see through flesh can also see through a cap."

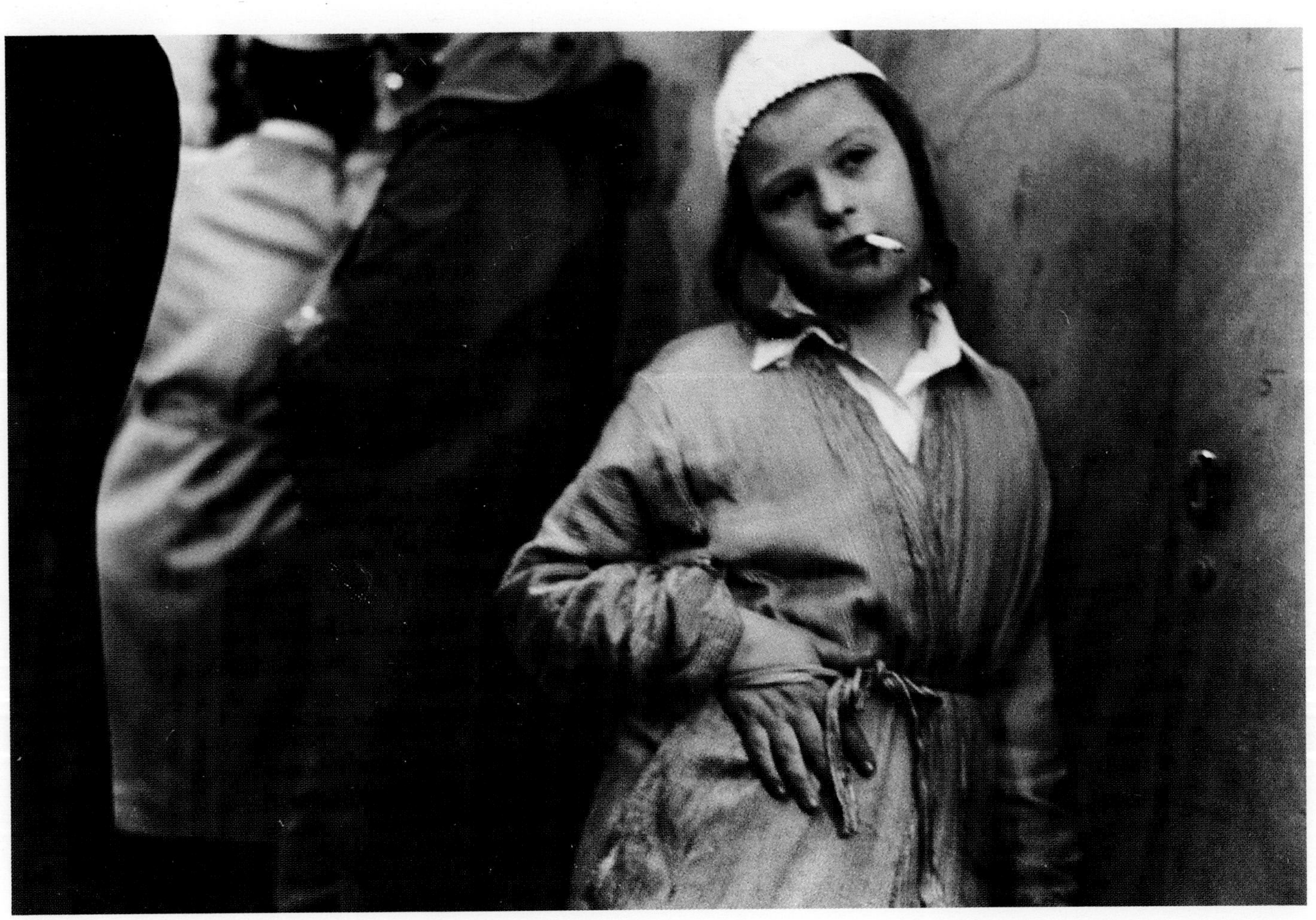

Rabbi Eliezer of Vizhnitz greatly loved his fellow man. Once when a Hasid came to him, the rabbi ordered that he be served a meal with meat and all kinds of delicacies. The Hasid, very apologetic, said, "I didn't come to eat and drink; I came to see the rabbi."
Rabbi Eliezer told him, "You should know that the soul does not descend into the world in order to eat or drink; nevertheless, if a person does not eat and drink, his soul leaves him."

Rabbi Nahman of Bratslav would say: "I am a beautiful and most remarkable tree, with marvelous branches, and I am literally implanted in the earth."

Rabbi Menahem Mendl of Kotzk asked a certain student: "Do you know how to study Torah?"
The student answered, "Yes."
"Do you know the meaning of the word 'Torah'?"
The young man remained silent.
"The meaning of the word," explained Rabbi Menahem Mendl, "is that the Torah teaches (*moreh* in Hebrew – from the same root as the word Torah) man. If you, however, think you are able to study alone, then the Torah has not yet taught you anything."

Once Rabbi Moses of Kobrin looked to the heavens and exclaimed: "Angel, angel. There is no great feat in living as an angel in the heavens. You don't need to eat or drink, to raise children and support them. Come down to the earth, and we'll see if you remain an angel."

All his life, Rabbi Israel Baal Shem Tov tried to remember the *nigun* – melody – of our forefather Jacob, and was unable to do so. This is what he told his confidantes: "In my first incarnation – when I was a sheep in Jacob's flock – I heard a most beautiful *nigun*. In that *nigun*, Jacob poured out his soul to his Creator, and the Holy One, Blessed be He, heard his voice and blessed his flock. It is said that that same *nigun* was sent by Jacob to his son Joseph through Joseph's brothers." The Baal Shem Tov added: "I was only privileged to hear it one more time. A certain shepherd sang it, and I almost turned into a sheep again."

When the Baal Shem Tov wished to move to the Land of Israel, he said: "I may be worthy of again hearing that *nigun* that came from the Land, and when I learn it again I will not forget it. Then, when that *nigun* becomes known, redemption will come to the Land."

When Rabbi Isaac Meir of Gur was six years old, someone said to him: "I will give you a gold coin if you tell me where God is to be found." The child answered him: "I will give you two gold coins if you tell me where He is not to be found."

A certain *tzaddik* told: "In a dream I once saw that I was brought to the Garden of Eden. There they showed me the ruined walls of Jerusalem on High, which is opposite Jerusalem on earth. Within the rubble and piles of dirt around and between the walls, I saw a man staggering and barely able to move. I asked: 'Who is that man?' They answered: 'It is Rabbi Israel Baal Shem Tov, who swore that he will not leave the area until the Temple is rebuilt.'"

There are three commandments that are performed properly even if one did not have the proper intention while performing them, and these are they: studying Torah, giving charity, and immersing oneself in the ritual waters of a *mikveh* .

Torah – because the Jew is studying it regardless;

Charity – because the other person gets the money regardless;

Immersion in the *mikveh* – because one removes one's ritual impurities regardless.

Rabbi Naftali of Roptchitz used to say: "No one ever had the better of me, except for a certain wagon driver.
"Once I saw an ignorant wagon driver singing and dancing on *Simhat Torah*, the festival which celebrates the completion of the entire cycle of Torah readings through the year.
"I said to him, 'My son, why are you so happy? What is so special for you? Do you then study the entire year?'
"'Rabbi,' he answered me, 'If my brother has a cause for celebration, shouldn't I be happy too? Isn't his joy my joy?'"

The Baal Shem Tov would say: "One must serve God in joy; not as a slave before his master, but in joy and exultation, as a son before his father."

The Hasidim of Rabbi Simha Bunim of Pshischa asked him: "When an author puts out a book, he usually adds a foreword. What foreword did God write to His Torah?" He answered them (quoting the *Ethics from the Fathers*): "*Proper behavior comes before the Torah.*"

Lord of the Universe! Permit me to always isolate myself so that I may be able each day to go out to the fields among the trees and grass, and there I will be able to remain alone and speak to You. This is my prayer to my Creator: to be able to speak there whatever is in my heart, and all the plants and grass and trees will give of their power toward my speech and prayer, until my prayer and my words will be utterly perfect because they are united with the power of all the plants. All will be included in my prayer. By this I will be able to open my heart to multiply my prayers and pleading and speech to You.

(Rabbi Nahman of Bratslav)

Rabbi Simha Bunim of Pshischa told: "The Seer of Lublin had better students than I, but I knew him better than did they. Once I came into his room when he wasn't home, and I heard whistling. It came from his clothes, that were singing his praise."

Rabbi Nahman of Bratslav would say: "One who wishes to really be a Jew, which means to ascend from one spiritual level to another, can only do so through *Eretz Israel* – the Land of Israel. This is the Land of Israel in the simple meaning of the term, with its houses and courtyards."

Rabbi Moses of Kobrin would say: "If it were up to me, I would get rid of all the books of the *tzaddikim*, the Hasidic leaders, for when one knows much Hasidic doctrine, his wisdom comes to exceed his good deeds."

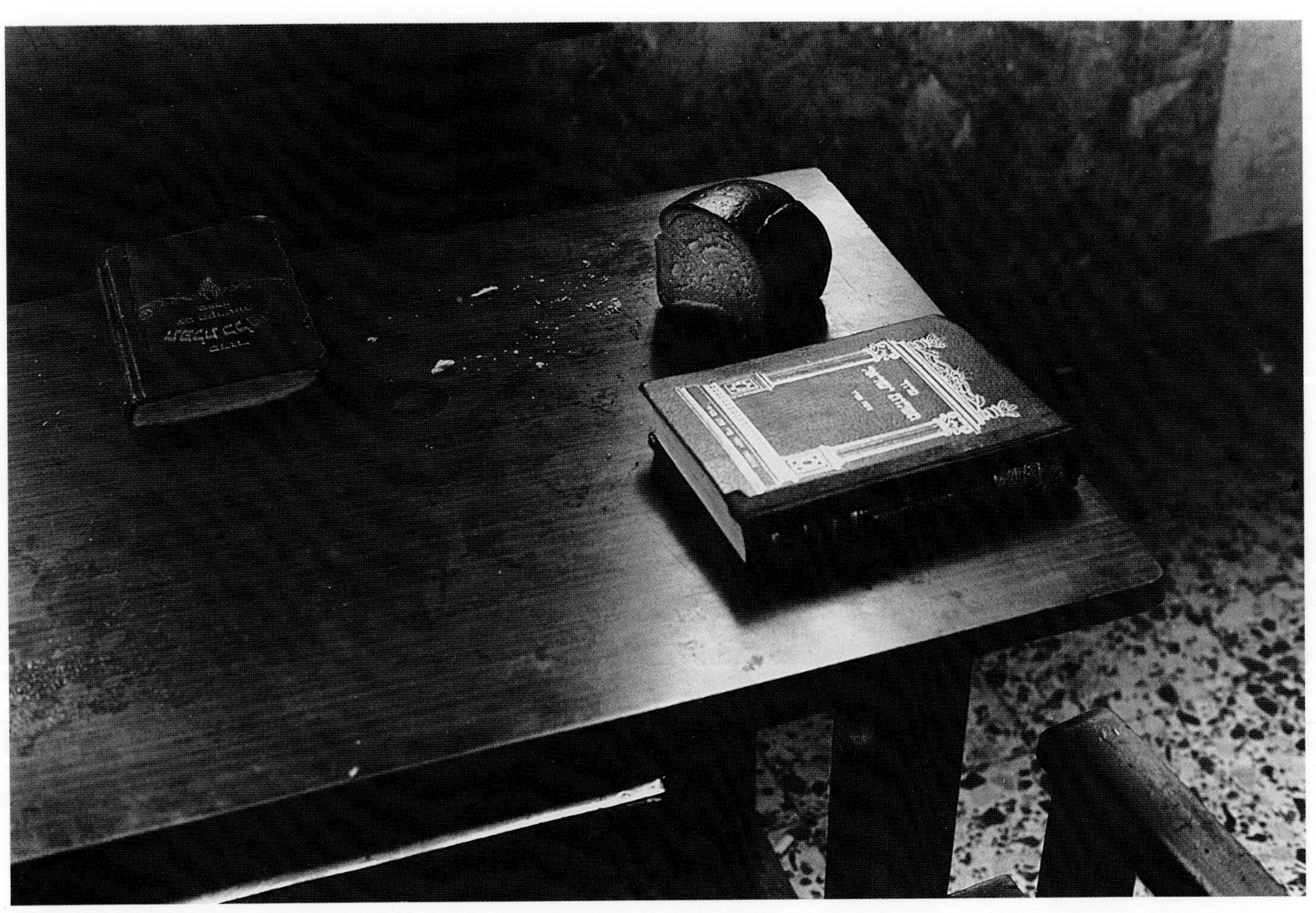

It is told: Rabbi Levi Isaac of Berdichev instituted that whenever a preliminary marriage contract, *Tennaim*, was written in his town, it would be phrased as follows: "The wedding will be, the Lord willing, on such-and-such a day in Jerusalem, the Holy City. Should, heaven forbid, our Messiah not come this year, the wedding will be in Berdichev."

A disciple asked Rabbi Israel Baal Shem Tov: "Why is it that a person who wishes to draw close to God sometimes feels as if He is moving away from him?"
The Baal Shem Tov answered him: "When a father wishes to teach his small son to walk, he moves away from him a little and stretches out his hands, so as to teach the child to be confident. When the child gets closer, the father again moves away, and by this means the son slowly learns how to walk."

When Rabbi Abraham Heschel of Apta served as the rabbi of Jassy, the members of the community sent him *mishloah manot*, the customary gifts of food exchanged on *Purim*, but included in the plate a number of gold coins as a gift. Rabbi Abraham Heschel took the coins and played with them for a long time. His family members, who knew that he hated to deal with money in any way, were amazed, and asked him: "Have you then changed your ways? We know that until now you would never even handle money, and yet here you seem to be playing with it so fondly."
Rabbi Abraham Heschel answered them: "Throughout the entire year I detest money and want nothing to do with it. Today we are commanded to give charity to the poor, but in the way I normally treat money, giving any to the poor would mean giving something I personally despise. I therefore decided that today I will make an effort to like money, and when I get to the stage of wanting to own it, I will give it away to the poor."

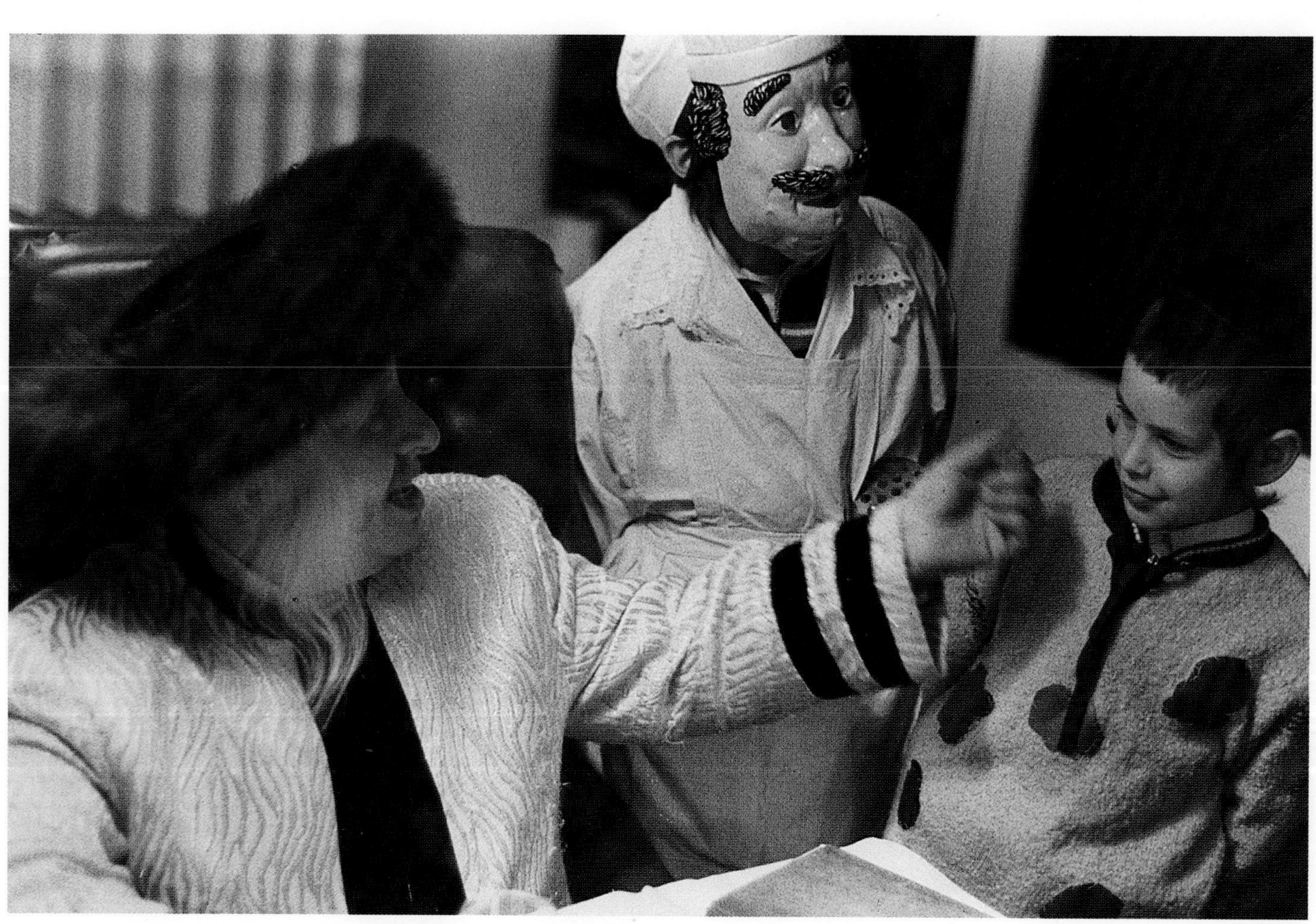

His Hasidim asked Rabbi Aaron of Karlin: "Why do Hasidim dance so much?"
He answered them: "When a person dances, he lifts himself a handsbreadth above the ground."

Rabbi Aaron of Kobrin would say: "There is no commandment that one must be happy, but nevertheless joy can bring about the fulfillment of all the other commandments.

"There is no prohibition against being sad, but sadness can bring about all the sins in the world."

Rabbi Nahman of Bratslav would say: "I only came to the world to draw Jewish souls closer to the Lord, but I can only do so with those who come to me and tell me what ails them."

A Hasid came to Rabbi Menahem Mendl and complained: "Rabbi, I have all types of terrible thoughts."

– "Such as?"
– "I am even afraid to say them. I feel absolutely terrible that I can even think thoughts for which no atonement is possible."
– "Tell me what they are."
– "Woe unto me! Sometimes I think that God doesn't exist."
– "So what do you care?"
– "What do you mean, 'What do you care?'" cried out the Hasid. "If there is no God, there is no purpose to the entire world!"
– "And what do you care if there is no purpose in the world?"
– "Rabbi, if there is no purpose to the world, what purpose is there to the Torah?"
– "And what do you care if there is no purpose to the Torah?"
– "Rabbi! If there is no purpose to the Torah, then there is no purpose to life – and that bothers me greatly!"

Rabbi Menahem Mendl said to the Hasid:

– "If that bothers you so much, you are a fine Jew, and a fine Jew is permitted to have such thoughts."

A man came to Rabbi Menahém Mendl of Kotzk and asked him how he could motivate his sons to study the Torah.
Rabbi Menahem Mendl answered him: "It states, 'You shall tell them to your children and children's children' (Deut. 4:9). If you really wish this, first you should study the Torah, and your sons will learn from you and copy your example, and so too your grandchildren. But if you do not study Torah, your sons will not do so, and will only tell their sons to study Torah without doing so themselves, and so on for future generations. This way, each will tell his sons how important it is to study the Torah, and soon the Torah will be forgotten."

After Rabbi Moses of Kobrin died, one of his disciples happened to visit Rabbi Menahem Mendl of Kotzk.
Rabbi Menahem Mendl asked him: "What was the most important thing to your rabbi?" He answered: "Whatever he was doing at that instant was the most important thing."

Rabbi Yom Tov Lippa Teitelbaum had many opponents in his town.
Once, when he was sitting at his table with his disciples, a large rock was hurled through the window into his home. The rabbi barely managed to duck, and was miraculously saved.
One of the disciples picked up the rock, turned it over and over, and exclaimed: "How large a rock it is. It is big enough to kill. How evil are those who threw it!"
"Heaven forbid!" the rabbi told him. "Jews cannot be suspected of throwing such large rocks. What happened is that many people threw small pebbles, and since each pebble said: 'I wish to hit the head of this righteous person,' they all united into this one rock."

Just before he died, Rabbi Simha Bunim of Pshischa heard his wife crying. He asked her: "Why are you crying? After all, the entire purpose of my life was to learn to die."

When Rabbi Israel Baal Shem Tov saw that a calamity was about to befall Israel, he would go to a certain place in the woods and remain alone. There he would light a fire and say a single prayer, and a miracle would happen and the evil decree would be averted.

Later, when his disciple, Rabbi Dov Ber, the Maggid of Mezrich, would need to ask for mercy for Israel, he would go to the same place in the woods and say: "Lord of the Universe! Listen to me. I do not know how to light the fire, but I can still say the prayer," and a miracle would occur.

And even later, Rabbi Moses Leib of Sasov would also go to the woods to save his people, and would say: "I do not know how to light the fire; I do not know the prayer; but I can find the place, and that must be enough." And it was enough: again a miracle would occur.

The time came for Rabbi Israel of Rizhin to avert the evil decree. He would sit on his couch, his head between his hands, and would speak to the Holy One, Blessed be He: "I cannot light the fire; I do not know the prayer; and I cannot even find the place in the woods. I can only tell this story. That must be enough." And it was enough.

When the Maggid of Mezrich was five years old, a fire broke out and burned down his parents' house. His mother grieved terribly. The little boy said to his mother: "Just because the house was burned, is that a reason for grieving so much?"
His mother answered: "Heaven forbid! I am not distressed about the loss of the house but rather about the loss of our genealogical table, which was burned in the house. Our genealogical table goes back all the way to Rabbi Yohanan the Cobbler."
"If that is so," said the little boy, "our genealogy will now begin with me."

Rabbi Zusya of Hanipol would bless each Jewish child he met: "May it be God's will that you be as healthy and strong as a gentile!"

Rabbi Menahem Mendl of Kotzk was asked: "Where is God?" He answered, "Wherever He is allowed in."

The Maggid of Mezrich was extremely poor. His wife constantly complained, but he never listened to her. Once she berated him, and he heaved a deep sigh.

A voice announced from the heavens: "Rabbi Dov Ber, since you sighed about your material plight, you have lost your place in the World to Come."

The Maggid was overjoyed, and exclaimed: "Now I am finally able to serve God without any thought of receiving a reward!"

Again a voice came from the heavens: "Dov Ber, your place in the World to Come has been restored."

The Holy Yehudi said: "When two Jews drink a '*l'chaim*' together in harmony and friendship, they see themselves as equals. Neither feels himself greater than the other."

PHOTOGRAPHS:

Jerusalem, 1983 . . . 3
Meah Shearim, 1983 . . . 5
Tel Aviv, 1984 . . . 7
Towards Safed, 1984 . . . 13
Safed, 1985 . . . 19
Bnai Brak, 1984 . . . 21
Jerusalem, 1986 . . . 23
Jerusalem, 1985 . . . 25
Jerusalem, 1983 . . . 27
Meah Shearim, 1984 . . . 29
Meah Shearim, 1985 . . . 31
Kiryat Malachi, 1986 . . . 33
Meron, 1984 . . . 35
Meah Shearim, 1981 . . . 37
Jerusalem, 1985 . . . 41
Safed, 1985 . . . 43
Jerusalem, 1986 . . . 45
Jerusalem, 1985 . . . 47
Jerusalem, 1986 . . . 49
Towards Meron, 1984 . . . 51
Jerusalem, 1986 . . . 53
Jerusalem, 1986 . . . 55
Meah Shearim, 1984 . . . 57
Jerusalem, 1986 . . . 59
Jerusalem, 1986 . . . 61
Jerusalem, 1984 . . . 63
Safed, 1984 . . . 65
Jerusalem, 1985 . . . 67
Jerusalem, 1986 . . . 69
Safed, 1984 . . . 71
Jerusalem, 1986 . . . 73
Safed, 1985 . . . 75
Jerusalem, 1986 . . . 78
Jerusalem, 1986 . . . 79
Jerusalem, 1986 . . . 81
Jerusalem, 1986 . . . 83
Jerusalem, 1985 . . . 85
Bnai Brak, 1983 . . . 87
Jerusalem, 1986 . . . 90
Jerusalem, 1986 . . . 91
Jerusalem, 1983 . . . 93
Jerusalem, 1986 . . . 95
Jerusalem, 1986 . . . 97
Safed, 1984 . . . 99
Jerusalem, 1986 . . . 101
Safed, 1985 . . . 103
Safed, 1984 . . . 107
Meron, 1983 . . . 109
Meah Shearim, 1983 . . . 111
Meah Shearim, 1986 . . . 113
Jerusalem, 1986 . . . 115
Kiryat Malachi, 1986 . . . 117
Jerusalem, 1985 . . . 119